DIGITAL DOTS

Work out the sums, then join up the dots in numerical order to reveal the mystery picture.

2×3= ●

● 8×6=

7×6= ●

9×5= ●

4×2= ●

10×4= ●

3×3= ●

3×4= ●

4×8= ●   9×4= ●   5×2= ●

7×2= ●

7×4= ●

5×5= ●

● 6×5=   5×4= ●

5×3= ●

6×3= ●

6×4= ●

3×7= ●

4×4= ●

3

Colour one half of each square. Use as many different ways as you can think of. Some lines have already been drawn to help you and the first one has been done for you.

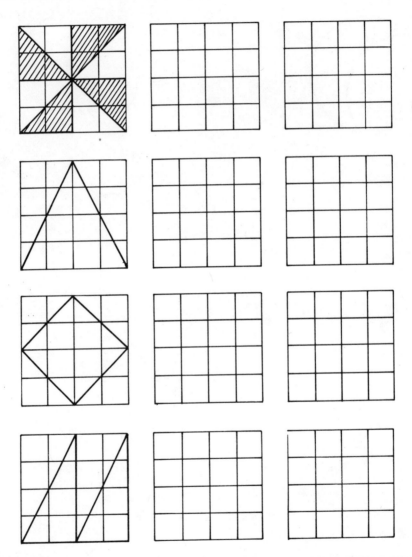

This activity aims to show the child that although the shape of the coloured areas may vary they all still represent one half. Try looking for other examples around you, for example: a half-full bottle of milk is still half full no matter at what angle it is tipped; a half-full box of chocolates is still half full no matter what the arrangement of the remaining chocolates.

PRACTISE TOGETHER SERIES

MATHSKILL 2

Games, puzzles and
investigations for maths
practice

Roger Hepworth

A Piccolo Original
Piccolo Books

...s a wide variety of mathematical puzzles, games and investigations ...timulate creative thinking and to motivate children in a way that ordinary ...an seldom achieve.

...ue of this type of activity has been clearly stated by Her Majesty's Inspectors and ...government report *Mathematics Counts* (Cockcroft, HMSO, 1982) which said, 'The ...ility to solve problems is at the heart of mathematics ... The idea of investigation is fundamental both to the study of mathematics and also to an understanding of the ways in which mathematics can be used to extend knowledge and to solve problems in very many fields.'

The age range on the cover is only approximate and should not be taken as a rigid guideline. If your child finds a particular activity difficult, give as much help as possible, or wait awhile until you think she may be ready to tackle it. The activities are graded from easier to more difficult through the book.

One of the most important aspects of this book is the conversation it will generate between you and your child as you work through the pages together. Such discussion should include not just the method used and the results obtained but also any false trails followed and mistakes made.

The notes in the boxes on most pages give guidance and hints to parents. (To avoid repeating *he/she* and *him/her* throughout, 'she' and 'her' are used in this book.)

Try to encourage your child to ask such questions as: What happens if I do this? Can I predict what is going to happen next? Could I have done the same thing a different way? Is there a pattern anywhere?

When starting a puzzle or investigation, it is important that all the results and calculations are clearly organized and written down. This will make any patterns easier to spot. Any ideas that occur should also be written down so that, if necessary, they can be followed up later. Be willing to follow some false trails and try not to say at the outset that it leads nowhere.

There is no set amount of time that should be given to an activity. Some may be over in a few minutes and others may take a day and at the end have raised more questions than answers.

Encourage the child to work in short bursts, at her own pace, and don't let the exercises become a chore. These activities are to be enjoyed. When they stop being fun, it is time for a rest and a change.

Many of the activities will be helped by the use of a calculator. A calculator means a child can obtain a much wider range of results accurately and quickly and so makes more difficult investigations accessible. It gives confidence to a child who is mathematically unsure, rather like arm-bands in a swimming pool, and aids the learning of tables and number bonds and leads to a better understanding of place value. Getting used to working with a calculator will undoubtedly help a child later on, in secondary school, where their use is widespread, even in examinations.

Parents should note that some calculators process operations in the order in which they are entered, rather than in the correct mathematical priority of $\div$, $\times$, $+$, $-$. This can affect the answer. For example: $2 + 4 \times 2$ makes 12, when processed in order of entry, but 10 when processed in correct mathematical priority ($4 \times 2 = 8 + 2 = 10$). Make sure, therefore, that the child is aware of the correct priority of operations and uses them as appropriate.

All the answers can be found on pages 31 and 32. On the inside back cover you will find a chart which tells you the mathematical areas covered in the book.

THE PAINTER'S PROBLEM

A painter has only three tins of paint. One blue, one red and one yellow. He wants to paint a street of houses but the owners are fussy. They say that every house must be different and that the roof must be one colour, the walls a second colour and the door and window a third.

The painter is worried about getting in a muddle so he decides to build a gadget to help him. From a piece of stiff card he cuts a triangle. Then from the middle he cuts another, smaller triangle. Finally he draws pictures on them and labels them like this.

FRONT OF TRIANGLE

BACK OF TRIANGLE

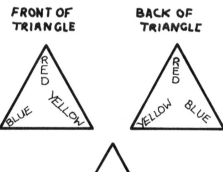

When he is ready to start painting, he puts the small triangle into the hole and this shows him which colours to use for each part of the house. When he has finished a house, he rotates the small triangle until it fits back in the hole. This gives him the colours for the next house. After a certain number of houses he turns the small triangle over.

Make the painter's gadget for yourself and use it to draw or paint some different coloured houses. How many houses can you paint?

WHAT IS IT?

To reveal the mystery picture, carefully colour in every area which has a number that will divide exactly by 7.

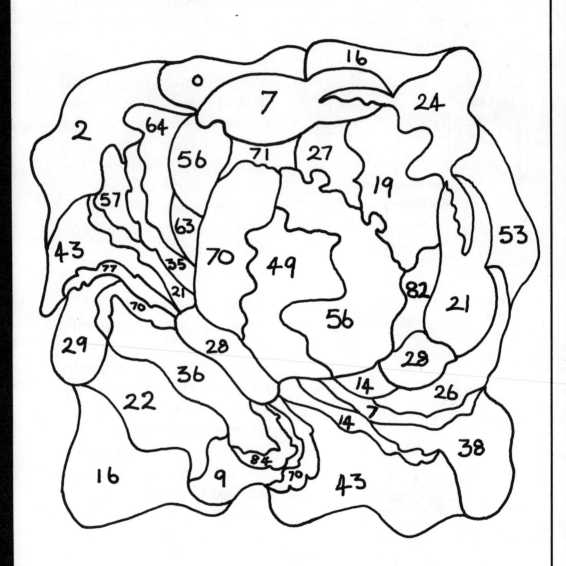

If dividing by 7 is too difficult for the child, then work out together and write down the 7 times table. Now look to see which numbers in the picture are in the list of products (answers). This procedure will also draw attention to the link between division and multiplication.

WORD SEARCH FOR MATHS WORDS

The words in this list have been hidden in the grid of letters.
Can you find them?

```
r i o s u m g e c e u e m s t a v t i
s g r p r b c y g y i h c i a y n a f
u y b t t m e k g n z p z h z g g k e
d v a e i x e g e g l m c h n b f e q
c i s g r s l u m m m e k o z i b x s
h u f q a w u k a y u h v u l x x a r
b f b f h m y q g y q l i r n c u w t
l u i e e o e d k e c g t z k r q a r
e q k b h r o b l o n g f i o q a y i
m a t b g i e e n e j o h b p b d y a
i x m z w a r n b b o t o m r l d t n
n m f z v a p d c y d g i w a i y h g
u n a f u j a c i e b r n p d f m j l
t j h q w y c h v v o o w r d i f g e
e p s y r v j i u b i x y o i c b g p
m w v n a f h t r o h d q d t q i w x
i e g c p u w s u c p j e u i k l v x
v e p m p w e m u m l t s c o d d l g
d k t j m a n n h u c e c t n m t j z
p b m m d s u b t r a c t i m n u x d
p m t g o d d o m t z g z e e y x w k
k o f t h t u x y k e o n x r i i q f
a w c h h s s f w l o m i x n g k y x
s u f g s p a f g m o w v k x j d e e
j a i s f e x n v n u m b e r d l l v
m e a d r t a f c y l i n d e r a n e
h m b a m v i h a w c k q u q c x z n
h w r b v m s p o k a d i g i t a a n
u m o q v v c c e f l x g t c s p a w
z e n a v v a r h e a k r t f b e f v
b t k v f q t f b b o e k f g h o e z
a r c e w e u w l d v q r s d r r j c
j e e c m k r a x u i w n i s u t b t
d p x o e d r b b v k a n o g n b q m
v n l a l e z g j q y w g i u p k s n
j i o e m b b m v i d w f o x f r k w
k q j u o g v j g k t i c y n z t n q
v v n o n r w r l r i k d o e a r l b
p a n q y g w o j a j y y n j z l d y
q g r z f s e t h o r i z o n t a l u
```

take away
difference
sum
square
oblong
divide
product
minute
week
metre
digit
figure
odd
diagonal
horizontal
angle
cylinder
mass
subtract
add
circle
triangle
cube
multiply
addition
hour
number
numeral
even
kilometre
vertical
area
count
height

ROUND AND ROUND

Start at 0. Count on 1. Join 0 and 1. Count on 1 again. Join 1 and 2. Carry on until you arrive back at 0. Colour the pattern you have made.

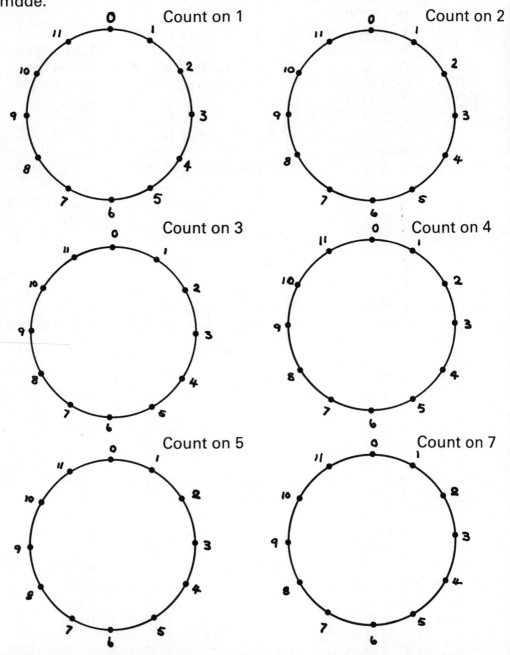

Count on 1

Count on 2

Count on 3

Count on 4

Count on 5

Count on 7

Can you explain why the last two patterns are more complicated?

TAKE A BALL

Draw out your own, larger copy of this diagram.

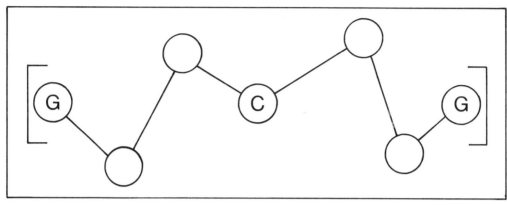

You will need: a counter or button to act as a ball. Place it on the centre spot.

This game is for two players.

Each of you starts with a set number of points, say 20. Then, in secret, you bid for possession of the ball by writing down the number of points you are prepared to pay. Then both of you reveal your bids and the player with the highest number of points moves the ball one spot towards the opponent's goal. In the event of a draw, the ball remains where it is.

The number of points bid by each of you is deducted from your total and then you bid again from your remaining points.

If all 20 points are used up without a goal being scored, that game is a draw and re-starts from the centre.

The aim of the game is to score a goal by out-bidding your partner enough times to move the ball on to the spot marked 'G'.

It is important that each player keeps both her and her opponent's score so that as points are used up she can begin to try to outwit the other player. This game is probably best played without a calculator and after a while the number of points started with can be increased to 50. A more difficult version, this time using a calculator, is to begin with one point each and to bid in units of not less than 0.01.

MULTIPLE PATTERNS

1	2	3	4	5	6	7	8	9	10
2	4	6	8	10	12	14	16	18	20
3	6	9	12	15	18	21	24	27	30
4	8	12	16	20	24	28	32	36	40
5	10	15	20	25	30	35	40	45	50
6	12	18	24	30	36	42	48	54	60
7	14	21	28	35	42	49	56	63	70
8	16	24	32	40	48	56	64	72	80
9	18	27	36	45	54	63	72	81	90
10	20	30	40	50	60	70	80	90	100

Colour in all the multiples of 5.

Colour in all the multiples of 4.

1	2	3	4	5	6	7	8	9	10
2	4	6	8	10	12	14	16	18	20
3	6	9	12	15	18	21	24	27	30
4	8	12	16	20	24	28	32	36	40
5	10	15	20	25	30	35	40	45	50
6	12	18	24	30	36	42	48	54	60
7	14	21	28	35	42	49	56	63	70
8	16	24	32	40	48	56	64	72	80
9	18	27	36	45	54	63	72	81	90
10	20	30	40	50	60	70	80	90	100

1	2	3	4	5	6	7	8	9	10
2	4	6	8	10	12	14	16	18	20
3	6	9	12	15	18	21	24	27	30
4	8	12	16	20	24	28	32	36	40
5	10	15	20	25	30	35	40	45	50
6	12	18	24	30	36	42	48	54	60
7	14	21	28	35	42	49	56	63	70
8	16	24	32	40	48	56	64	72	80
9	18	27	36	45	54	63	72	81	90
10	20	30	40	50	60	70	80	90	100

Colour in all the multiples of 3.

Colour in all the multiples of 6.

1	2	3	4	5	6	7	8	9	10
2	4	6	8	10	12	14	16	18	20
3	6	9	12	15	18	21	24	27	30
4	8	12	16	20	24	28	32	36	40
5	10	15	20	25	30	35	40	45	50
6	12	18	24	30	36	42	48	54	60
7	14	21	28	35	42	49	56	63	70
8	16	24	32	40	48	56	64	72	80
9	18	27	36	45	54	63	72	81	90
10	20	30	40	50	60	70	80	90	100

1	2	3	4	5	6	7	8	9	10
2	4	6	8	10	12	14	16	18	20
3	6	9	12	15	18	21	24	27	30
4	8	12	16	20	24	28	32	36	40
5	10	15	20	25	30	35	40	45	50
6	12	18	24	30	36	42	48	54	60
7	14	21	28	35	42	49	56	63	70
8	16	24	32	40	48	56	64	72	80
9	18	27	36	45	54	63	72	81	90
10	20	30	40	50	60	70	80	90	100

Colour in the multiples of your choice.

A multiple of a number is produced by multiplying that number by another, e.g. 3×1=3, 3×2=6, 3×3=9. So 3, 6, and 9 are all multiples of 3.

NETS

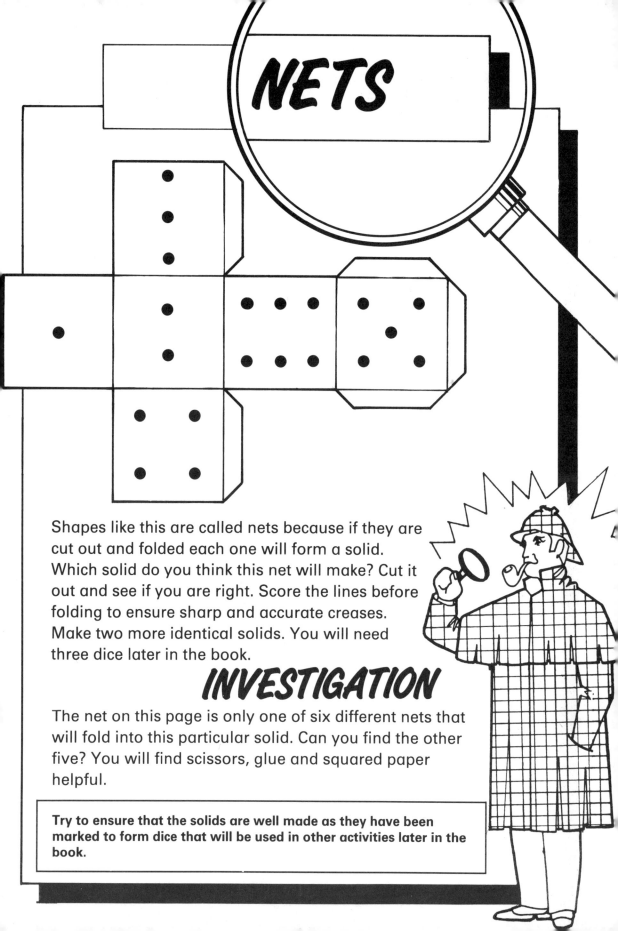

Shapes like this are called nets because if they are cut out and folded each one will form a solid. Which solid do you think this net will make? Cut it out and see if you are right. Score the lines before folding to ensure sharp and accurate creases. Make two more identical solids. You will need three dice later in the book.

INVESTIGATION

The net on this page is only one of six different nets that will fold into this particular solid. Can you find the other five? You will find scissors, glue and squared paper helpful.

Try to ensure that the solids are well made as they have been marked to form dice that will be used in other activities later in the book.

TREASURE TRAIL

Mad Maths Murry the infamous pirate has hidden his treasure somewhere on the island. Can you decode his message and find it?

START 6+4	33:E 72−6	18:T 16+11	67:− 60+24	42:T 14+67	29:O 31−19	44:B 47−4	94:E 36−12
28:M 15+8	38:E 76−4	88:T 100−1	10:U 5+4	30:Z 100−6	14:E 36+5	32:T 93−4	31:Y 98−9
34:P 60−6	60:M 60−2	43:Y 36−17	35:M 14+7	19:− 34+18	37:P 41+9	81:R 55+7	39:L 50+10
72:− 26+18	9:N 12−4	36:H 19+11	27:− 18+14	90:F 22−8	58:− 33+9	40:G 56+3	51:H 25+48
45:D 19+19	99:R 100−6	66:− 18+19	46:S 23+32	62:E 43−5	73:E 76−9	8:D 20−6	84:S 52+36
41:R 32−5	47:O 72+6	52:T 43+8	24:A 41−13	89:H 27+6	85:J 13+73	23:END ——	50:A 48−9

Reveal the message by answering the sum in the square marked 'start'. Then find the square with the answer and write down the letter in the space for the message. This square will lead you on to the next.

PROBLEM FAMILIES!

A father offers his two children a choice of how to receive their holiday money during the next 12 days. They can either:

1 Receive £30 all in one go, or

2 Receive 1p on the first day, double that, i.e. 2p on the second day, double that, i.e. 4p on the third day, and so on for 12 days.

How would you choose to receive your money and why? Be careful, your parents may just take you up on your choice!

FASHION FIGURES

Mary is a very fussy girl when it comes to deciding which clothes to wear. She insists on having a different outfit for every school day and one more set of clothes for the weekend.

Mary's mother says that this will cost far too much but Mary says that she can do it with only five pieces of clothing, if they are a mixture of blouses and skirts.

Is Mary right? If so, what mixture of blouses and skirts must she have?

If Mary wanted a different outfit for every day of a 12 day holiday what is the least number of skirts and blouses that she would need?

PALINDROME

In mathematics a palindrome is a number which reads the same in both directions, e.g. 66, 121, 23632. If you follow the instructions in this flow chart carefully, you will discover a method for producing such numbers.

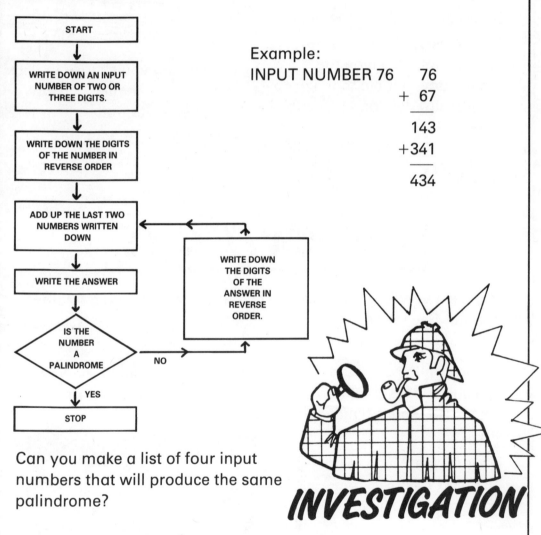

START

WRITE DOWN AN INPUT NUMBER OF TWO OR THREE DIGITS.

WRITE DOWN THE DIGITS OF THE NUMBER IN REVERSE ORDER

ADD UP THE LAST TWO NUMBERS WRITTEN DOWN

WRITE THE ANSWER

WRITE DOWN THE DIGITS OF THE ANSWER IN REVERSE ORDER.

IS THE NUMBER A PALINDROME

NO

YES

STOP

Example:
INPUT NUMBER 76

$$
\begin{array}{r}
76 \\
+\ 67 \\
\hline
143 \\
+341 \\
\hline
434
\end{array}
$$

Can you make a list of four input numbers that will produce the same palindrome?

INVESTIGATION

Which two digit number takes the longest to produce a palindrome?

A calculator is very helpful here, as it will permit the child to experiment quickly with a far wider range of numbers.

LAND GRAB

On the island of Notalot the precious mineral Silranium has just been discovered. The island has been surveyed and divided into numbered plots. The higher the number the richer the plot.

The Governor of Notalot, Sir Evenless, has ordered that prospectors must throw three dice for the plots.

They may claim a plot by using the scores on the three dice in any order, together with the four operations ($\div$, $\times$, $+$, $-$), to make a total equal to the number on a plot.

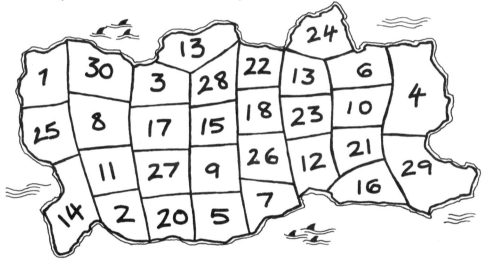

So, for example, suppose the dice show 3, 6 and 2:
then $3+6-2=7$ claims plot 7
  or $3\times6+2=20$ claims plot 20
  or $6\div2+3=6$ claims plot 6
and so on.

A record of each claim is kept by pencilling in the prospector's initial on the plot claimed. Each plot may only be claimed once.

After 10 turns each, the prospectors add up the value of their plots. The winner is the prospector with the most valuable total.

A calculator will speed up the game for younger or less confident children by enabling them to try out a variety of combinations quickly.

RICKY ROBOT

Ricky has been drawn by plotting his co-ordinates. Some examples are shown on the drawing to help you, e.g. (1,8), (1,5), (3,8) etc.

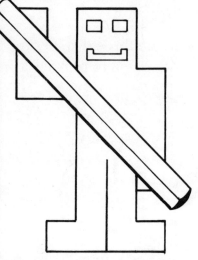

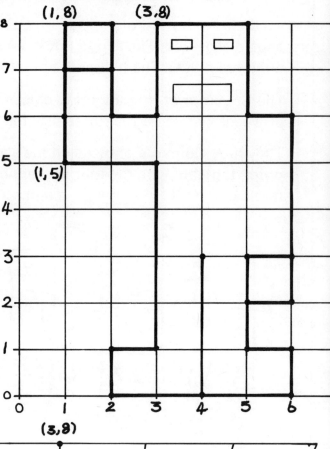

Try drawing him again by plotting his co-ordinates on the grids provided.

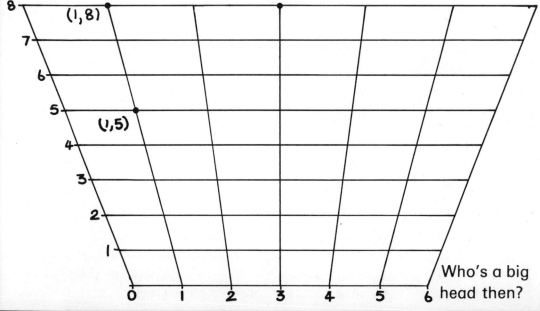

Who's a big head then?

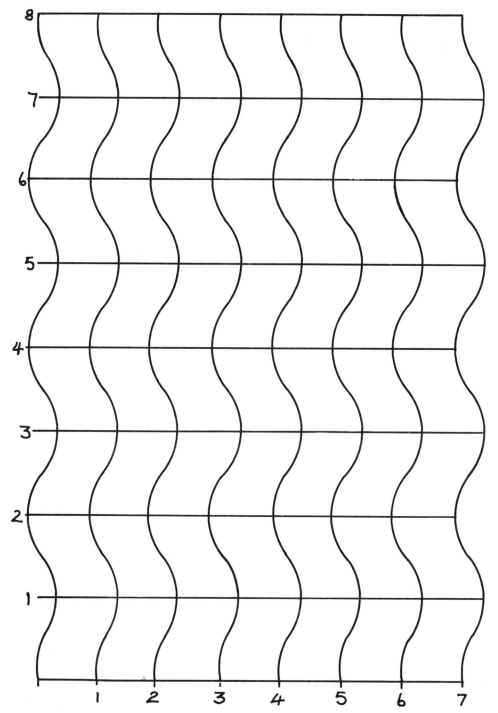

Write how you think Ricky feels now ....

It is important to remember that co-ordinates are plotted by reading
horizontally first, then vertically. An interesting effect can be obtained by using
squared paper and doubling the numbers of each co-ordinate, e.g. (2,8)
becomes (4,16), etc.

THE GREAT DIVIDE

Is it possible to tell, just by looking at a number, whether it will divide by another number? Try the following investigation and find out for yourself.

With a calculator, divide these numbers by five and then sort them into the two sets shown: 40, 18, 16, 25, 97, 935, 110, 44, 1980, 173, 219, 511, 802, 1235.

Set A
Numbers that divide
exactly by five.

40

SET B
Numbers that do not
divide exactly by five.

18
16

> **It may be necessary to show the child how to tell when the calculator display shows that a number has not divided exactly, i.e. there will be digits other than zero after the decimal point.**

What do you notice about the last digit of the numbers in set A? Can you write a rule to help someone test a number for division by five?

....

....

....

Now try dividing these numbers by three, then sort them into two sets as before: 12, 20, 44, 65, 93, 53, 105, 231, 540, 306, 117, 79, 118.

SET A
Numbers that divide
exactly by three

_____
_____
_____
_____
_____
_____
_____

SET B
Numbers that do not
divide exactly by three

_____
_____
_____
_____
_____
_____
_____

Next add up the digits of each number in set A and divide by three again, e.g. 231→2+3+1=6→6÷3=2.

Now do the same with the numbers in set B. What do you notice about these two new sets of answers?

Can you write a rule to show how to test if a number will divide by three?

How about division by four?

Look at these two sets of numbers.
Set A: Numbers that divide exactly by 4: 16, 20, 424, 536, 360, 172.
Set B: Numbers that do not divide exactly by 4: 17, 23, 345, 574, 233, 191.

Try dividing just the tens and units digits of each number by four:
e.g. 1128→28÷4=7. What do you notice about the answers?

Can you explain to a partner how to check if a number will divide exactly by four?

If the child is really interested in this activity she can try finding tests for divisibility by 6, 8 and 9 as well. (They are similar to those already covered.) 7 is best avoided as it is too difficult.

THAT'S NOT FAIR!

On day Tricky Jim told his friend Harry about a new game he had discovered. Carefully he explained the rules.

Each of them would throw two dice in turn and add up the score shown on each dice.

If the score were 2, 3, 4, 5, 10, 11 or 12, Harry would win a point. If the score were 6, 7, 8, or 9 then Tricky Jim would win a point. The first player to score nine points would be the winner.

Harry was so certain he would win, he told Tricky Jim he would give him his best marble if he lost.

Pretend to be Tricky Jim and Harry and play the game five times. Keep the result of each throw in a matrix like this.

SCORE	6	8	5	7	2	7	9	8	3	2
TRICKY JIM	✓	✓		✓		✓	✓	✓		
HARRY			✓		✓				✓	✓

Poor Harry. He realised afterwards that he had been tricked but he could not work out how. Can you investigate and find out for him?

INVESTIGATION

It is important that the dice used are in good condition so that they are unbiased. If the child is interested she could try to work out the rules for a similar game in which the score on the two dice are multiplied instead.

WHAT'S NEXT?

1. 2, 4, 6, 8, …, …, ….

2 12, 10, 8, 6, …, …, ….

3 1, 2, 4, 7, 11, …, …, ….

4 3, 6, 12, 24, …, …, ….

5 4, 8, 12, 16, …, …, ….

6 1, 4, 9, 16, 25, …, …, ….

7 32, 26, 20, 14, …, …, ….

8 1, 1, 2, 3, 5, 8, …, …, ….

9 2, 5, 3, 5, 4, 5, 5, …, …, ….

10 1, 9, 2, 8, 3, 7, …, …, ….

11 1, 121, 1331, …, …, ….

12 0.1, 0.3, 0.5, …, …, ….

13 1, 0.8, 0.6, 0.4, …, …, ….

14 0.25, 0.5, 1, 2, …, …, ….

15 100, 121, 144, …, …, ….

16 1, ½, ¼, …, ….

17 20, 40, 30, 19, 39, 29, 18, …, ….

18 1.3, 1.5, 1.7, …, …, ….

19 1.5, 0, 1.3, 1, 1.1, 2, 0.9, 3, …, …, ….

It is often helpful to look at the differences between the numbers in the series,
e.g. 9, 7, 5, has a difference of two each time so should continue 3, 1. More
difficult series are sometimes made by combining two or more series, e.g. 1, 2,
3 and 5, 6, 7 becomes 1, 5, 2, 6, 3, 7.

NUMBER CROSS

Can you fit the numbers into the square?

CLUES

Across	Down
28	15367
49638	24
51	8902
5286	481
733	5734
905	99
419	600

This one is rather more difficult.

CLUES

5261	41287
5348	48217
5624	203
5012	205
94	2473
96	91
98	4326
375	92
42187	54841

A careful record of which numbers have already been used should be kept.
Encourage the child to work logically rather than by continual trial and error.

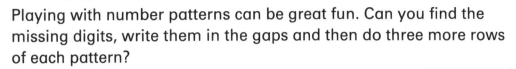

NUMBER PATTERNS

Playing with number patterns can be great fun. Can you find the missing digits, write them in the gaps and then do three more rows of each pattern?

$1 \times 9 + 2 = 11$
$12 \times 9 + 3 = 111$
$123 \times 9 + \_ = 1111$
$123\_ \times \_ + \_ = 1111\_$

....
....
....

$9 \times 9 + 7 = 88$
$98 \times 9 + 6 = 888$
$9\_7 \times 9 + \_ = 8888$
$\_8\_\_ \times \_ + 4 = \_\_\_\_\_$

....
....
....

$1 \times 8 + 1 = 9$
$12 \times 8 + 2 = 98$
$123 \times 8 + \_ = 987$
$1\_3\_ \times \_ + 4 = \_\_\_\_$

....
....
....

$8 \times 4 = 8 \times 2 \times 2$
$8 \times 6 = 8 \times 3 \times 2$
$8 \times 8 = 8 \times 4 \times 2$
$8 \times 10 = \_ \times \_ \times 2$

....
....
....

$1 \times 8 = 10 - 2$
$2 \times 8 = 20 - 4$
$3 \times 8 = 30 - 6$
$\_ \times 8 = \_\_ - \_$

....
....
....

$1 \times 98 = (1 \times 100) - 2$
$2 \times 98 = (2 \times 100) - 4$
$3 \times 98 = (3 \times 100) - 6$
$4 \times \_\_ = (\_ \times 100) - \_$

....
....
....

An interested child can be encouraged to seek other similar patterns. A calculator should be used for this activity as it will enable the child to carry out a large number of calculations accurately and within her attention span.

KLONDYKE CLAIM

Imagine you are a gold prospector in the days of the Klondyke gold rush. When you arrive you see this notice. Quickly you realise that your best chance of striking it rich is to mark out as much digging space as possible. What shape should your claim be for this to happen?

KLONDYKE CLAIM RULES

NO CLAIM SHALL HAVE A PERIMETER GREATER THAN 24m. *by order* MARSHALL

Here are some earlier prospectors claims. Can you do better?

4

32 SQUARES

8

8   **8**

28 SQUARES

8

6   **38 SQUARES**

9

The claims do not have to be straight sided. A thin piece of wire 24cm long laid on squared paper will help mark out the claims. Where part squares are involved a reasonably accurate count can be made by ignoring all part squares less than ½ and by counting as 1 all part squares equal to or greater than ½.

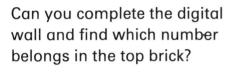

DIGITAL WALLS

Can you complete the digital wall and find which number belongs in the top brick?

Row 3: | 4 | | 11 | |
Row 2: | 3 | 1 | 7 | 4 | 5 |

| 9 | 12 |
| 9 | 5 | 1 | 8 | 4 | 3 | 2 |

Can you find a quicker way of getting the answer than having to add up each pair of bricks in turn?

For example:

```
        6+3+3+2
    6 + 3   3 + 2
    6     3     2
```

INVESTIGATION

CLUE
Try with a small wall first and write the sums rather than the answers in each brick.

CALCUCROSS

You will need a calculator for this activity. Complete the calculation for each clue, then turn the calculator upside down to read the answer as a word.

Clues across

1. Stare hard ★ 47076×8
5. Short hello ★ $\sqrt{196}$
6. Sharp surprise ★ 2000+2506
7. Ask for help or money ★ 1000−362
9. Garden tool ★ 912÷3
10. Name ★ 28867×11
11. Window ledge ★ 80^2+1315
16. Musical instrument ★ 154×20
17. Pom poms ★ (220007+4110)×24
18. Slippery fish ★ (700−63)×9

Clues down

1. Holy book ★ 200^2−2182
2. Silly laugh ★ 2400^2−380081
3. Chicken producer ★ 331×3
4. Footwear ★ 203×3×5+50000
8. Part of a shoe ★ 193×38
9. . . . and she ★ 100−66
10. A chunk of wood ★ 200+500−93
12. Not well ★ 1000−229
13. Misplace ★ $\sqrt{90000}$×10+507
14. Earth ★ 1421×5
15. American pig ★ 1000÷2+104

CONCENTRIC SHAPES

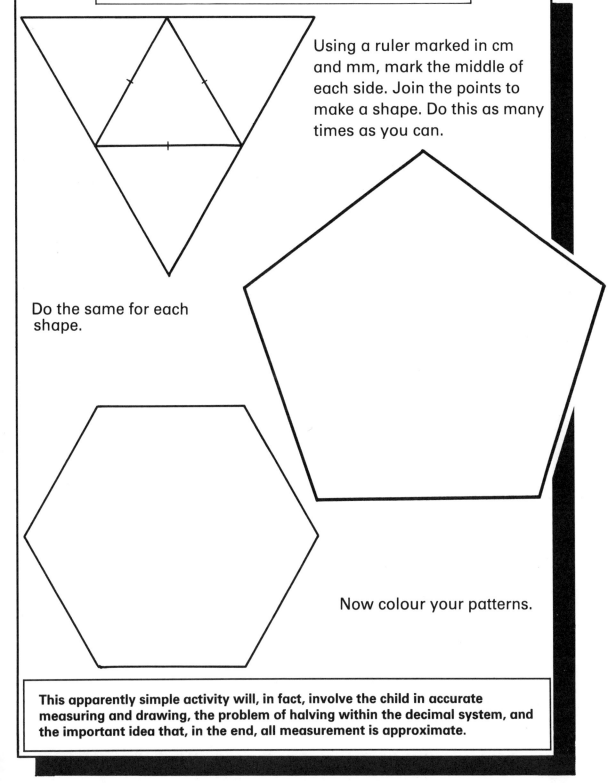

Using a ruler marked in cm and mm, mark the middle of each side. Join the points to make a shape. Do this as many times as you can.

Do the same for each shape.

Now colour your patterns.

This apparently simple activity will, in fact, involve the child in accurate measuring and drawing, the problem of halving within the decimal system, and the important idea that, in the end, all measurement is approximate.

The fascinating pattern at the top of p. 29 is based on the pattern of products (answers) from the 3× table. Read carefully to see how it was built up.

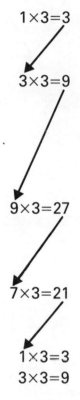

The first line starts at 3 (marked A) because . . . $1 \times 3 = 3$

Now take the unit digit of the answer (3) and multiply that by 3 . . . $3 \times 3 = 9$

The answer is 9 so this is the second point on the line (marked B).

Again take the unit digit of the answer (9) and multiply that by 3 . . . $9 \times 3 = 27$

The unit digit of the answer (7) now gives the third point on the line (marked C). $7 \times 3 = 21$

Continue this process until you reach the end of the grid, e.g. . . . . $1 \times 3 = 3$
$3 \times 3 = 9$

The second and third lines begin again at the left at 6 and 9 and continue as follows.

Second line	Third line	Fourth line	Fifth line
$2 \times 3 = 6$	$3 \times 3 = 9$	$4 \times \ldots$	$5 \times \ldots$
$6 \times 3 = 18$	$9 \times 3 = 27$		
$8 \times 3 = 24$	$7 \times 3 = 21$		
$4 \times 3 = 12$	$1 \times 3 = 3$		
$2 \times 3 = 6$	$3 \times 3 = 9$		
$6 \times 3 = 18$	$9 \times 3 = 27$		

The pattern is completed by starting on the left each time and working through the remainder of the 3× table up to 9×3.

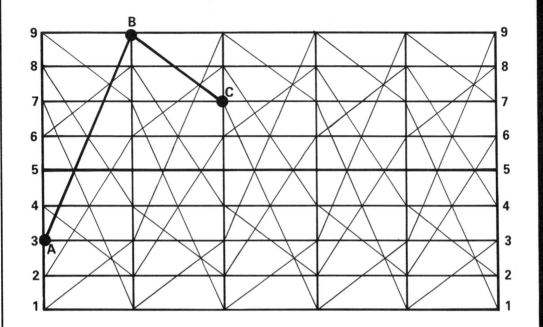

Try plotting the nine times table in the same way on this lattice, then complete the pattern by colouring it in. The first two lines have been done for you.

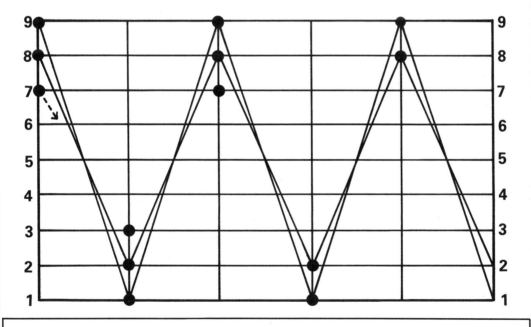

If the child is interested she can draw out her own grids and plot the remaining tables. The 5 and 10 times tables are best avoided as they do not produce particularly interesting patterns on this occasion.

SUM SUMS

Here are some sums with a difference. You will really have to put on your thinking cap.

1. Only one of these answers can possibly be correct. Can you say which one it is?

256
+1_5   **a.** 364   **b.** 461   **c.** 351   **d.** 361

2. Using the information given in the first sum, can you fill in the missing answers without working out the whole sum each time?

$27 \times 24 = 648$ $27 \times 12 =$

$24 \times 27 =$ $27 \times 6 =$

$648 \div 27 =$ $648 \div 12 =$

$648 \div 24 =$ $648 \div 6 =$

3. Can you tell which answer in each pair will be the bigger without working them out?

a. 1286 **b.** 1286   **a.** 92   **b.** 92
   +127   +137   ×5   ×6   **a.** $124 \div 4$ **b.** $124 \div 6$

4. Three of these answers are wrong. Can you say which three?

a. 24_   **b.** 24_   **c.** 24_   **d.** 24_
   ×10   ×5   ×4   ×3
  2046   1204   968   733

5. Arrange the digits, one in each box, so that the difference between the two numbers is as great as possible.

1, 2, 3, 4, 5, 6.

The questions on this page have been carefully designed to test a child's *real* understanding of our number system, rather than simply to follow mechanical processes. Ask the child to explain fully how she achieved her answers as this will tell you a great deal about her current level of understanding.

ANSWERS

Digital dots: (p.3) The mystery picture is a space rocket.

A ½ is a ½ is a ½: (p.4) Open ended.

The painter's problem: (p.5) The painter can paint six houses without repeating a colour scheme.

What is it?: (p.6) The mystery picture is a crab.

Word search for maths words: (p.7) Self checking.

Round and round: (p.8) Self checking. As each pattern should be symmetrical the line should eventually return to zero. 2, 3 and 4 are all factors of 12 and so divide into it exactly. Therefore, going round the circle once only returns you to zero. 5 and 7 are not factors of 12 and so it is necessary to continue round the circle a number of times until a number is reached which is a multiple of 12 and also a multiple of 5 or 7.

Take a ball: (p.9) Open ended.

Multiple patterns: (p.10) The answers require only simple multiplication and can be checked by the parent as necessary.

Nets: (p.11) These are the six nets of a cube:

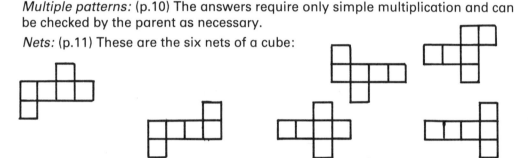

Treasure Trail: (p.12) The message reads: UNDER THE PALM TREES BY THE STREAM.

Problem families: (p.13) Provided you are prepared to wait for your money, choice 2 is the best, as by the twelfth day you will have received a total of £40.95.

Fashion figures: (p.13) Mary is correct. She needs two blouses and three skirts or vice versa. For twelve days she will require three blouses and four skirts or vice versa.

Palindromes: (p.14) Open ended, except that 89 or 98 are the two two-digit numbers that take the longest to produce a palindrome using this method.

Land grab: (p.15) Open ended.

Ricky Robot: (p.16) Ricky should still be recognizable but he will have been distorted along the lines of the grid.

The great divide: (p.18) Numbers which divide by 5: 40, 5, 935, 110, 1980, 1235.
Rule: A number which divides by 5 will have 5 or 0 as the last digit.
Numbers which divide by 3: 12, 93, 105, 231, 540, 306, 117.

Rule: A number which divides by 3 is a number the sum of whose digits when added up will divide by 3.
Rule for numbers dividing by 4: The last two digits will divide exactly by 4.

That's not fair: (p.20) The game is not fair because overall Tricky Jim's scores are more likely to occur than Harry's. For example, the score 7 can be created in six different ways: (1,6) (2,5) (3,4) (4,3) (5,2) (6,1). This means that it has a greater chance of coming up than the score of 5, which can only be created in four ways: (1,4) (2,3) (3,2) (4,1). If you look at all the scores you will see that although Tricky Jim has fewer winning scores, they are more likely to occur.

What's next? (p.21) **1.** 10, 12, 14. **2.** 4, 2, 0. **3.** 16, 22, 29. **4.** 48, 96. **5.** 20, 24, 28. **6.** 36, 49, 64. **7.** 8, 2. **8.** 13, 21, 34. **9.** 5, 6, 5. **10.** 6, 4, 5. **11.** 14441, 155551. **12.** 0.7, 0.9, 1.1. **13.** 0.2, 0.0. **14.** 4, 8, 16. **15.** 169, 196, 225. **16.** 1/8, 1/16. **17.** 38, 28. (20, 40, 30, 19, 39, 29, 18, *38, 28, 17*) **18.** 1.9, 2.1, 2.3. **19.** 0.7, 4, 0.5.

Number cross: (p.22)

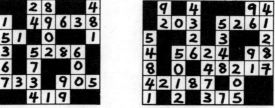

Number patterns: (p.23) The continuation of the pattern should make these self checking.

Klondyke claim: (p.24) A *circle* encloses the greatest area for any given perimeter.

Digital walls: (p.25) The top brick of the small wall should contain the number 70. The top of the larger wall should contain the number 294. A quicker way of calculating the answer is to discover how many times each number is added in on its way to the top. For a wall with five bricks at its base, it is 1, 4, 6, 4, 1. Now the answer can be calculated by multiplying each of the numbers in the base line of bricks that number of times, and adding together the answers: $(3\times1)+(1\times4)+7\times6)+(4\times4)+(5\times1)=70$.

Calcucross (p.26)

Concentric shapes: (p.27) Open ended.

Patterns from numbers: (p.28) Open ended.

Sum sums: (p.30) **1.** d. No matter which digit is placed in the empty box, it cannot produce any of the other three answers. **2.** This question checks on the child's understanding of the operations of multiplication and division and the relationship between them, i.e. if $27\times24=648$, then 27×12 must equal half as much because 12 is half of 24. Also, if $27\times24=648$, then $648\div24=27$, etc. **3.** b, b, a. **4.** a, b, and d are incorrect as no matter which digit is substituted for the box, it will not produce the answers given. **5.** 654 and 123 produce a difference of 531.